In Your Light
We See Light

Heaven's Supernatural Victories
Are Ready to be Released

Mary Donna Hankla

Endorsed by Dr. P. Douglas Small of Project Pray!

Book Cover by Sermonassist

Illustrations by Eddie Sheffield III

1st edition 2023

ISBN: 979-8-9880394-0-2

Library of Congress Control Number
2023909064

KJV – King James Version. Scripture quotations marked in "KJV" are taken from the Holy Bible, King James Version, Cambridge, 1769

AMP – The Amplified Study Bible. Scripture quotations marked in "AMP" are taken from the Amplified Study Bible, Copyright © 2017 by Zondervan, Grand Rapids, MI 49496.

DEDICATION

So many people have given time and effort to enhance my spiritual walk with the Lord. I would not want to forget to mention any of them.

"More valuable than gold are the prayers and support of others."—Donna Hankla

To my mother, Mary Shepherd, I give honor. In addition, I give thanks to J.C. Shepherd. My mother always provided encouragement.

My father, Don Sturgill, who has since gone on to heaven, I am grateful for the many fly-fishing trips we had together.

To my husband, Kenneth Hankla, and my son, Chris Hankla, both of whom have spent countless hours putting together this book. Chris provided the technological support needed to launch it.

Kim Slemp, my sister, and her husband Danny, gave me the confidence to reach for this dream.

Dan Sturgill, my brother, and his wife Cherie, as well as my sister-in-law Kathy Sheffield and her husband Eddie uplift me in my efforts.

My niece, Katrina Sheffield, is my faithful supporter.

My mother-in-law, Louise Hankla, and my father-in-law, Bill Hankla, who have gone on to heaven, for their inspiration.

Eddie Sheffield III, my talented nephew, provided expert graphics.

Bishop Preston Mathena and his wife, Kathy, mentored me as I pursued my call to ministry. They are proven intercessors.

Pastor Stacy Cope gave me the courage to attempt to write a book.

Larry and Kay Smith taught me when I was a teenager. They were my 4-H leaders as well as Bible teachers.

Ron and Sandra Fowler from South Carolina are my intercessors. They have prayed for several miracles, many of which happened just in time.

The Appalachian Conference Board and staff constantly provide support. Ron Fredericks and Larry Meadors, both on the board, are strong in faith and inspire others to pursue Christ.

I can assure you that if your name is not mentioned here, it is certainly written in my heart.

TABLE OF CONTENTS

FOREWORD

Starting in Chapter 1, you can clearly see that at an early age, Donna was chosen by God to be a prayer warrior in His army. I have had the pleasure of knowing Mrs. Donna since my childhood. I have witnessed her intercede in prayer for her community, the Appalachian Conference, IPHC, our nation, the world, others, and me. Donna's heart beats for God, His kingdom, and His will. She is truly a beacon of light that shines throughout her life's testimony and her words written in this book. As you read, you will see her love and compassion. She shines God's light wherever He opens the doors of opportunity to do so.

You will discover that miracles occurred through Donna's passion for praying to God. Moreover, you will also realize that she and her family experienced miracles because she passionately gave to God as well. In Chapter 7, Donna shares testimonies about different cats in her life. I am highly allergic to cats and for that reason, I've never been too fond of them. However, as Donna wrote her testimonies about the cats, I found myself wiping tears from my eyes and face. She converted me in this chapter and inspired me to find a place in my heart to love cats. Likewise, I pray that her testimonies throughout this book will convert others to love Christ and build their faith in Him.

To be honest, I think every Christian should take the time to read Donna's heartfelt words and learn from her life experiences, so they can grow spiritually and find encouragement in their communication with God the Father, Son, and Holy

Spirit. Donna is more than just a prayer warrior in God's army; I see her as a general! Donna, I salute you for your tremendous contributions to the kingdom of God.

Pastor Stacy C. Cope
Pastor & Author
Lead Pastor of Tower of Refuge Church

www.testimoniestold.com

I am always amazed at who God chooses and uses to change a culture. I have known Donna Hankla for over 30 years and no one I know has been more faithful to prayer. Her simple position of faith and prayer, as well as her passionate pursuit of God, have impacted all who know her. In this book, she shares the miracle stories of God's work in her life. The theme of the book is Psalm 36:9, "In your light shall we see light." May this book bring greater revelation of God's ways and work in your life!

Bishop K. Preston Mathena
Superintendent Appalachian Conference, IPHC

In Your Light, We See Light, is a reminder that prayer is the context for illumination and insight. Wisdom is a name for the Spirit. He reveals things we might not otherwise see. He whispers secrets.

One of the key roles of the church is to be an intercessory community for the city – the nation and the nations. We have too often bent prayer backward to benefit us. Petition, prayer for personal needs, is legitimate. Indeed, it is how we demonstrate dependence on God. It is the way we invite God into the deficits of daily life. Without it, we are proud and self-sufficient. "We have not" because we don't pray (James 4:3).

Yet, prayer was never meant to stop with a petition. It is bigger than our slice of pain or our set of problems. Healthy prayer moves from seeking God's hand to seeing God's face, and that illuminated face enhances insight. It changes everything, including us. And then, healthy prayer feels the heart of God for a lost world – this is intercession. It is the noblest use of prayer. It is the duty of prayer.

In intercession, we stand with God, with Christ, enabled by the Spirit, becoming the Father's representative on the earth through prayer. In this middle, we join God's sufficiency to man's necessity. That mysterious connection allows the current of heaven to pulse through us to touch someone – and open their eyes to salvation and more light. Sometimes it delivers them from bondage or holds them up during a siege of spiritual warfare.

When Paul wrote to Timothy, he urged him to establish the church on a foundation of prayer, to "pray for kings and those in authority," indeed, for "all men" that they might be saved (1 Timothy 2:1-4). No prayer – no breakthroughs. No prayer – barren altars. No prayer – no community transformation. No prayer – blindness to the light. You will never know the importance of your intercessory labor until you view the earth from heaven – what a stunning and impactful role.

Isaiah the prophet wondered when, in Judah, there was no intercessor. God must wonder today why we don't pray – especially for the lost, for cities, and nations. The word "wonder" could have been translated as appalled or even horrified. This is an anthropocentric description of God. He is horrified, mystified, and baffled as to why Judah, His chosen people, were not interceding. Why did they not see the importance of intercessory prayer, of standing in the middle, representing Him, giving Him voice and visibility on the earth, allowing His power to change the hearts of kings and people of power and influence? Why?

In the absence of intercession, the nation was falling apart. This really is astounding. We never give this level of importance to prayer. The problem was not that "the Lord's hand" was too short to reach them or that He could not save them (Isaiah 59:1). No, the problem was two-fold – their sins and their prayerlessness. And those two are bound together.

"Your wrongdoings have caused a separation between you and your God, and your sins have hidden His face from you so that He does not hear" (Isaiah 59:2). He will not give you a "hearing" in His courtroom. Bloody hands. Deceitful lips. Wicked tongues. Intercessory prayer is the prayer of a watchman. It is meant to expose us to sin's impact, to the deadly effect of wickedness, to sinners trapped in bondage from which they cannot extricate themselves. In prayer, we see them. In prayer, reflecting God's divine light, they see. The role of intercession is sobering in its effect on us and salvific in its impact on others. In Your Light We See Light.

Intercession first appears in Genesis, where Adam is told to guard the garden (Genesis 2:15). He was to "take care" of the garden, but that was only possible by prayer. He didn't, of course, and the serpent invaded the sacred space and seduced humanity. He is doing that today in families and cities, even in churches. From the beginning, God is teaching us the protective nature of prayer and the restraint of prayer against evil.

When there is no intercessor, a culture begins to fall apart. Thinking is cloudy. Devastation and destruction are too common (Isaiah 59:7). The way of peace is no longer familiar. Justice is rare. Paths are crooked (Isaiah 59:7-8). Darkness settles over the land. Spiritual blindness is common. Behavior becomes beastly – juxtaposed against depression and melancholy (Isaiah 59:11-12). What a picture of America.

Wrongful, harmful acts are multiplied. God is denied, and faith is abandoned. Oppression and revolt become common (Isaiah 59:12-13). The lack of integrity is demonstrated in one lie laid on top of another. Righteousness doesn't have a chance. Truth stumbles. The godly become targets (Isaiah 59:14-15). And "The Lord saw, and it was displeasing in His sight." He saw it then, and He sees it now.

And then, He notes the cause, "There was no one... not one to intercede" (Isaiah 59:15-16).

The absence of intercessory, missional prayer results in social and moral chaos. We can't see how an intercessor could be so powerful and important in the scheme of things. This is the moment when Isaiah reveals God's plan. He, God, will pray. He, God, will become the intercessor. He will wrap Himself in flesh, and with His own arm, He will bring salvation (Isaiah 59:16-17).

Adam had failed as had Noah. Abraham's seed had failed. The priests of Israel had failed. So God put on the breastplate of righteousness and the helmet of salvation and came to the earth – to pray! And even now, Jesus "ever lives to make intercession" (Hebrews 7:25). We are never more like Jesus than when we join Him in intercession. He is weeping over our cities – can we join him in intercessory prayer? He is seeking the lost – and that salvation process unwraps in our prayer partnership with Him.

"I would that men would pray everywhere, lifting holy hands without wrath or doubting" (1 Timothy 2:8). Here is the church, out of the building, acting as priests – a kingdom of priests, with lifted hands, blessing our cities. We must invite God to come. We bless our cities open to the good news. We don't pray for judgment – wrath, nor do we doubt the efficacy of prayer. Such prayer, Paul says, leads to "tranquil and quiet lives" lived in "godliness and dignity."

Prayer, like incense wafting through the city, changes the ethos of a city. We have no idea. And it results in salvation!

(1 Timothy 2:4). Men come to the knowledge of the truth. It is not preaching that is the first step in evangelism-mission; it is prayer. The Great Commission is subordinated to one thing. "Go into all the world and preach" (Mark 16:15), but first, pray – wait for the empowerment of the Spirit (Acts 1:4-5).

Charles Finney, the great evangelist of the second great awakening era, partnered his evangelism with the intercessory prayer ministry of Father Nash and Abel Clary. The two men went into cities in advance of Finney and prayed, often in shifts, twenty-four hours a day. They fasted. They groaned. They agonized over the city, sometimes walking its perimeter. They rarely attended the meetings when Finney arrived, continuing to pray for him as he preached. And God touched whole communities.

When we learn to partner intercession and evangelism-mission, then and only then will we have the level of breakthrough for which we long.

The great apostle Paul recruited the Colossian church to be his intercessory partner. "Pray," he urged them, "that a door might be opened for me to preach the gospel" (Colossians 4:2). He was not content to preach through a closed door. Only prayer opens the doors of closed hearts to the gospel. Only passionate intercessory prayer will open America and its cities to the gospel to see the harvest for which we all long.

I am thrilled to write this foreword and commend Bishop Preston K. Mathena and the WIN (World Intercessory Network) team of the International Pentecostal Holiness Church.

Yes, God hears. Yes, souls are awakened to the love of God. Yes, the darkness is pushed back. Yes, light and glory still come. Yes, the hardest hearts are made soft – all through the agency of intercessory prayer. Hats off to a conference superintendent who values the prayer and mission partnership and identifies and encourages intercessors. Commendations to intercessors who stay on the wall and cry out day and night.

To Bishop Mathena and the WIN team – God still has every tear you have shed in prayer. He keeps them in bottles in heaven (Psalm 56:8). And prayers that you have prayed, to which He has said "yes," and you have not seen the breakthrough are not lost or forgotten. Your counterparts in heaven, the elders, hold them in bowls, awaiting the time they will be mixed with fire from heaven's altar and their power released into the earth (Revelation 8:3-5).

Your lonely times are not in vain. Heaven sees. Heaven is praying with you. Jesus is agreeing with you – that the church will triumph, that the kingdoms of this world will become the kingdom of God's dear Son and that a final harvest is coming.

Keep praying! And may the stories of this book inspire an army of intercessors in every congregation.

Dr. P. Douglas Small, Project Pray
Project PRAY!
P. Douglas Small
704-938-9111 (Office)
704-996-5091 (Cell)
PO Box 1245; Kannapolis, NC 28082-1245

8600 William Ficklen Dr, Charlotte, NC 28269
www.projectpray.org
www.projectpraypublications.org

INTRODUCTION

"Let the redeemed of the Lord say so, Whom He has redeemed from the hand of the adversary" (Psalm 107:2 AMP).

The testimonies of God's intervention in the lives of others give powerful inspiration. Such stories strengthen our faith. As we listen, hope arises in our hearts. For if God did great miracles in their lives, He can also intervene in ours!

The heavenly scenes that appeared to me were filled with purpose, and I do not take my ability to see in the spiritual realm lightly. I desire to give God honor as I reveal those scenes in this book.

Many times, I prayed to God saying, "Let me see what You are saying, God." And I reminded Him of key scriptures to support my request.

"Call to Me and I will answer you, and tell you (and even show you) great and mighty things, (things which have been confined and hidden), which you do not know and understand and cannot distinguish" (Jeremiah 33:3 AMP).

"Open my eyes (to spiritual truth) so that I may behold Wonderful things from Your law" (Psalm 119:18 AMP).

The Prayer That Brought Swift Victories

My prayer life exploded with victories as I learned to pray this prayer. The scripture reference is Psalm 36:9. I quote and pray this scripture: "In Your light we see light!" My prayer was to see things the way God wanted me to see them. Also, I asked God for His light to scatter the darkness.

17

This prayer is for you too. When you pray for God's light, victories are within your reach.

CHAPTER 1

THE PATH OF LIFE

On that autumn evening, I was delighted to feel the refreshing bursts of wind blowing into my room through the open window. I decided to take a break from my work and gazed outside. The college campus was surrounded by hills now aglow with the vibrant colors of the trees. It was truly a pleasant sight to behold.

Anatomy tests and assignments were due the following morning. My two roommates and I were studying. I had been doing so tirelessly until my eyes became heavy with sleep. But I wouldn't sleep for long.

Without warning, a brilliant light illuminated our room. I got up and peered outside. It was dark—yet, light engulfed the room.

The other girls in the room also woke up and, like me, sensed God's presence among us. All of us shared a deep belief in the power of prayer, so we took turns saying our prayers aloud. Suddenly, at around midnight, we were jolted by the sound of loud marching outside the window. It was as if cadets were practicing drills right outside. Despite the intensity of the sounds, when we looked outside, no one was in sight.

Moved by this inexplainable event, I asked the Lord about the marching and sensed the following response:

"This is the army of the Lord. You will join this army in due time. It will be an army of intercessors. You will meet many prayer warriors."

MORE!

Indeed, these events were supernatural, and we were all amazed by the experience. When we began to settle back into sleep, the room started to shake so violently that the bed literally moved a few feet! No sleep for us, we continued to pray until dawn.

WHAT HAPPENED?

We were all fairly young girls who had been attending the campus Bible groups. The supernatural experience had a profound impact on us, and we knew we had to respond. As a result, I became more zealous to pursue a life of prayer, and another roommate became a Methodist minister.

BRIGHTER

"But the path of the just is like the shining sun, that shines ever brighter unto the perfect day" (Proverbs 4:18 NKJV).

I started on the path in the above scripture when I was seventeen. Our family worked hard. Both Dad and Mom held jobs. And then there was the farm. I would never trade those days of working on the farm. The land flourished with beans, strawberries, squash, and fields of tobacco. As hard as it was, the farm work kept our family together. We appreciated each other.

Often, I looked at the majestic Appalachian Mountains with their tall peaks. Mount Rogers, the tallest mountain in Virginia, was just miles from us. I wondered what lay beyond those mountains and what would take me to the other side to a life more reputable than farming. Would it be education? Would it be hard work?

No, and no! It would be prayer! I followed the path of prayer, for it was flooded with light!

PRAYER WAS NECESSARY

That year, 1975, our family was going through some serious troubles, despite attending church regularly. We knew that we needed someone to pray for us, so I decided to go on a search to find that person.

Luckily, there was a Bible study offered before school in our county, so I decided to attend in search of someone who could pray for our family.

As I walked into the room, I saw numerous faces filled with joy, and hands raised in praise. This was a new experience for me, as people were praying with great passion.

Then, someone approached me and began to pray for me. It was surprising to realize that many people have never had someone pray for them.

That encounter initiated a journey of prayer for my family, and I often wondered if all of my family members would turn to God. But to my delight, the day eventually came when I saw them all committed to their faith.

FAMILIES TODAY

Many families today are facing various troubles. Some are struggling with financial shortages, while others are dealing with frequent fights and arguments. Testy teenagers can often test the nerves of their families, and illnesses can strike without warning. Now more than ever, families need hope, and they need prayer.

IF YOU WANT TO SEE—JUST ASK

The prayers for me changed my life. As I reflected on Scripture, I noticed that Jesus often taught in parables using things the people could see. So that led me to the idea, why not ask God to let me see? I decided to ask and was amazed at the results. I said: "Our Father in heaven, let me see what You are saying. Let me see what to pray about. Let me see how to intercede."

This scripture verse transformed my prayer life, and it can do the same for you: "For with You is the fountain of life; In Your light we see light" (Psalm 36:9 NKJV).

A FUTURE MISSIONARY

It would not be long before my prayer would be answered. As a young seventeen-year-old, I was influenced by those students who prayed with passion. And I learned to pray with great expectation.

One day, I was walking around the house praying over the pictures of family members. I was drawn to a picture of my sister. As I prayed for her, I knew a missionary would come from her family in the future. I could sense it!

My sister, Kim, has a family with three children. Her oldest daughter served overseas to aid refugees, particularly in South Sudan where she helped the poor and afflicted people. She worked with young children and mothers who struggled to feed their families.

Kim is a devout Christian and takes her children to church on a regular basis. Her strong faith serves as an inspiration to her entire family.

STAY GROUNDED ON GOD'S WORD

Truly, it's amazing to experience God's presence and to see as the Holy Spirit allows. In such an atmosphere, intercession flows with great power. However, it's important to follow certain rules to protect ourselves.

Make sure to ask that your encounters with seeing and praying are confirmed with scripture. Remember the basic principles of hearing God's voice.

- Does your encounter agree with God's Word?
- Does your encounter agree with God's character?
- Is your encounter being confirmed by messages that you are hearing from church or Bible study?
- Does this encounter bring glory to God and not to you?

"My sheep hear my voice, and I know them, and they follow me" (John 10:27 KJV).

SHEEP THAT HEAR

Sheep are fascinating animals. As a child, I loved watching my grandfather take care of his sheep. Whenever I visited the farm, he would let me pet them and even put me on their backs.

He would always count his sheep to ensure that none were lost. To do this, he stood on a hill, waved his white handkerchief, and yelled: "Sheep, sheep, here sheep!"

Often, the sheep would be lying under shade trees to avoid the hot sun. But when they heard my grandfather's voice, they would get up and come to him. They knew his voice, and they knew that he cared for them.

YOU TRY

My grandfather wanted me to learn all about farming, so he handed me his handkerchief and said, "You try to call the sheep." He explained that when the sheep come to us, we would give them food and water.

It seemed simple to me, so I took the handkerchief and waved it, then shouted the same words that he said. But those sheep just looked at me and wouldn't budge. They paid no attention to me at all.

This taught me a valuable lesson about prayer: when I have to make major decisions, I must pray and listen carefully to hear the Lord's voice.

LAID OFF

"For from days of old no one has heard, nor has ear perceived, Nor has the eye seen a God besides You, Who works and acts on behalf of the one who (gladly) waits for Him" (Isaiah 64:4 AMP).

This verse proved to be a key resource for me during a difficult time in my life.

Receiving the dreaded pink slip and being laid off is something no one wants to experience. Sadly, it happened to me after working at a hospital for nearly fourteen years doing a job I loved. Cardiac rehabilitation was my area of expertise, and I found it truly rewarding to watch my clients recover from major surgery. Now, I had to look for another job. What would I do?

PRAY

As I prayed about the situation, the Holy Spirit instructed me to wait quietly in God's presence for forty minutes every morning for thirty days. No talking. No distractions. Just waiting!

After thirty days of waiting, a job opportunity opened up for me that was very similar to what I had been doing. The staff there was considerate and kind. Waiting confidently upon God brings His help and intervention. There is great power in committing your situation to God and then resting in Him.

"For he that is entered into his rest, he also has ceased from his own works, as God did from his. Let us labor therefore to enter into that rest, lest any man fall after the same example of unbelief" (Hebrews 4:10-11 KJV).

SOMETIMES WE NEED TO SEE

A picture is worth a thousand words! This means what we see can convey a message or evoke feelings more effectively than words. For example, we are inspired by seeing pieces of art that feature tall mountain peaks or beautiful beaches. Likewise, our faith is inspired and strengthened when the Holy Spirit allows us to see. Consider the prophet Jeremiah when he suffered in prison.

King Zedekiah punished the prophet with imprisonment because of his message. God gave Jeremiah a message for the king, but Zedekiah didn't like it and responded to Jeremiah in anger. However, God gave Jeremiah instructions that would encourage him.

"Call to me and I will answer you, and tell you (and even show you) great and mighty things, (things which have been confined and hidden), which you do not know and understand and cannot distinguish" (Jeremiah 33:3 AMP).

You can use the preceding scripture as a prayer. Are you facing a situation that seems impossible? Like Jeremiah, do you feel alone? God has some wonderful things to show you!

DARK IN THE PRISON

It was dark in the prison. But God's Word would bring light and hope! Jeremiah would soon be rescued. God would not let him perish there. An Ethiopian man named Ebedmelech heard about Jeremiah's imprisonment and made a decision to take action to free the prophet. He approached the king and pleaded for Jeremiah's release. The king listened and gave the command to draw Jeremiah up from the dungeon.

SEE THE GOODNESS OF THE LORD

"I had fainted, unless I had believed to see the goodness of the Lord in the land of the living" (Psalm 27:13 KJV).

I have often prayed this scripture. King David's perseverance has encouraged me! David was anointed to be the king of Judah by the prophet Samuel. However, he had to wait until King Saul finished his reign. After David killed the giant named Goliath, King Saul became very jealous of David. When David returned from war, the women celebrated by singing and dancing.

They said, "Saul has slain his thousands, and David his ten thousands." This saying enraged King Saul (1 Samuel 18:7-9).

One day, as David played comforting music for King Saul, he faced the anger of the king. King Saul threw a javelin at David with the intent to pin him against the wall. But David fled twice from these murderous attempts (1 Samuel 18:8-18).

Finally, the day came when David was crowned king of Judah. He saw the goodness of the Lord in the land of the living.

FINANCIAL ATTACKS

This prayer has seen me through job lay-offs in the health field prior to COVID-19. It has also helped me weather a few financial setbacks. Like King David, I have experienced the goodness of the Lord in the land of the living.

In the future, I will also see the goodness of the Lord in the land of the living.

CHAPTER 2

FLAMES ABLAZE

"Flames ablaze" is the best way to describe what was seen during a time of prayer. It was a heavenly scene of something burning fiercely. This event triggered me to join the prayer movement with other churches in the community.

When this occurred, I was participating in all-night prayer meetings at the Voice of Praise Church in Bluewell, WV. Bishop Preston and Kathy Mathena were the church leaders who were devoted to prayer. They are true intercessors. I have seen many answers to their prayers.

I kneeled and prayed for the community at the altar, not expecting any type of heavenly scene. But suddenly, I saw flames ablaze from tiny bonfires throughout the mountains.

BONFIRES IN THE MOUNTAINS

In the dark of the night, bonfires burned, shedding a bright light on the surrounding areas. What was also interesting was that the bonfires were arranged in a circle formation. As for the exact number, it was difficult to count them all. However, upon seeing them, it became clear that they represented individual prayer warriors offering up prayers for the community.

"Lord, I call upon You; hurry to me. Listen to my voice when I call to You. Let my prayer be counted as INCENSE before You; The lifting up of my hands as the evening offering" (Psalm 141:1, 2 AMP).

These scriptures confirm the value of our prayers!

DANCING FLAMES OF BONFIRES

The flaming bonfires seemed to burn in a circle formation for a long time. They were so amazing to look at that my eyes were glued to them. As they shined with great power, they also moved back and forth. Were they dancing as they burned?

These bonfires seemed to have personalities. They appeared to be full of joy as they burned. Also, they stayed within their boundaries. They did not jump ranks. They did not spread fire to the surrounding brush. They were content to burn within their own territory.

ANGELS ALSO

While I did not see angels in this heavenly scene, I could sense their presence. Even though the night was dark, there were illuminating figures. The bonfires were not the only sources of light, as splashes of brightness could be seen across the sky. The night seemed to be full of action as if it were alive.

ONE LARGE BONFIRE

Suddenly, the scene changed. These flaming bonfires leaped to the center of the circle. Now, there was one huge bonfire. The fire was so bright that it lit up a map of the entire community. When I saw this, I was inspired to call the community churches together for times of prayer.

"Unto the upright there ariseth light in the darkness: He is gracious, and full of compassion, and righteousness" (Psalm 112:4 KJV).

NIGHTS OF GLORY

I was not alone as I walked in obedience to the commission of calling the churches together for prayer. Bishop Preston Mathena and the prayer leaders from the Voice of Praise provided much support.

It was a simple plan. I would call the pastors of the local churches and invite them to a prayer meeting. Pastors were invited to preach and lead in prayer. We prayed for the Mercer County, WV community, the nation, and Israel. Worship songs were part of each service.

These powerful prayer meetings occurred about twice a month for a year. God's presence was noted by an atmosphere of peace and joy and participants were greatly strengthened in their faith.

SPIRITUAL WARFARE

As you can imagine, I did not pursue these meetings without conflict. There were intense periods of spiritual warfare. But God always protected and provided. As I said earlier, often, I could sense that I was not alone.

During times of uncertainty, I persevered. Prayer meetings were organized and not canceled despite attempts to delay or stop them. In the midst of the challenges, the intercessors remained determined to continue the prayer vigils.

"Praying always with all prayer and supplication in the Spirit, and watching thereunto with all perseverance and supplication for all saints" (Ephesians 6:18 KJV).

THE AFTERGLOW

Amazing spiritual events occurred during the community prayer meetings. Often, I came home exhausted and fell into a peaceful sleep, sensing God's presence. Oh, what a glorious feeling it was to experience His presence.

In my sleep, there was an overwhelming sense of peace, accompanied by delightful aromas that filled my senses, as if I were in a garden of spices. These experiences made me eagerly anticipate each nightly prayer meeting, knowing I would be blessed with God's presence when I returned home.

"The aroma of your oils is fragrant and pleasing; Your name is perfume poured out; Therefore the maidens love you" (Song of Solomon 1:3 AMP).

TOUCHED BY AN ANGEL

One night, after returning from a prayer meeting, I was exhausted and had to lie down on the couch. I closed my eyes, but I was not yet asleep. I tried to muster up enough strength to prepare supper. Suddenly, I sensed a presence near me. Despite feeling no fear, I opened my eyes to see what it was.

For a brief moment, I sensed a very large angel, clothed with garments of warfare. I could tell he had a sword, and that he was protected with brass-type clothing. I forgot about my exhaustion. Not knowing what to do, I stayed very still.

Then the angel reached out his hand and touched my right shoulder. He did not linger but left quickly. Scripture tells us angels are ministering spirits (Psalm 103:20).

KEYS HANGING FROM JESUS' WAIST

"And when I saw him, I fell at his feet as dead. And he laid his right hand upon me, saying unto me, "Fear not, I am the first and the last. I am he that lives, and was dead; and, behold, I am alive forevermore, Amen; and have the KEYS of hell and death" (Revelation 1:17-18 KJV).

During a prayer meeting held by Mercer County Aglow, a heavenly scene appeared before me.

Jesus was walking through Mercer County with keys around His waist. I knew it was Mercer County because I could see the map.

As He walked throughout the county, the visible, large keys dangled from His waist. I knew they represented authority and that keys were also used to open and shut doors.

It seemed as if Jesus had turned His head and glanced at me with a smile on His face.

PRAYER WALKING

This scene encouraged me to call a group of intercessors together to prayer walk in important areas of the county. We did prayer walks around churches, schools, interstate intersections, and businesses. We prayed for God's protection upon the county and visited several church lots to pray for them to thrive.

"Behold, I give unto you power to tread on serpents and scorpions, and over all the power of the enemy: and nothing shall by any means hurt you" (Luke 10:19 KJV).

A CHOIR OF ANGELS

During this time of corporate prayer meetings with the community churches, I experienced several heavenly scenes.

One morning, I went to the Voice of Praise Church, in Bluewell, WV at 9:00 a.m. I was waiting in the lobby for a meeting with the pastor when I heard very loud singing coming from the sanctuary of the church. Who could be singing at this time of day? The choir practiced at night. Also, the lights were turned off in the sanctuary. How could they be singing in the dark?

The singing was so delightful that I was attracted to the tunes. I could not help myself. I opened the doors of the sanctuary, hoping my presence would not frighten the singers. However, I saw nobody in the church. Yet, on the right side of the church, near the ceiling, I heard the sound of a choir singing. There was also an illuminated light in that area, and they continued to sing even with my presence.

41

Of great interest, the songs were not sung in the English language. I tried to figure out the language, drawing upon my knowledge of Latin and Spanish. However, these languages were not what the angels were singing. It was a heavenly language. Sounds of heaven were being sung throughout the church.

"When the morning stars sang together and all the sons of God shouted for joy" (Job 38:7 AMP).

EYES OF JESUS GLOWED AS A FLAME OF FIRE

"His head and his hairs were white like wool, as white as the snow; and his eyes were as a flame of fire" (Revelation 1:14 KJV).

This is another scene I experienced during the prayer meetings at the community church. One night, I attended a revival meeting at a church that regularly participated in prayer meetings. As part of the service, there was a time of sitting at the altar. It was during this time that a heavenly scene appeared, which surprised me.

Jesus' face was hovering over the pulpit. His eyes were upon the congregation. I strongly felt that He was looking directly at the hearts of people. My heart was also in His line of sight.

His eyes were like fire. Indeed, fire flashed from both of His eyes. I was not afraid but a wave of reverence covered me. It was like being washed over by a wave in the ocean.

The sermon that night was about building upon the foundation, which is Jesus Christ (1 Corinthians 3:11–15). Some people build with gold, silver, and precious stones. Others build with wood, hay, and stubble.

I wanted to build my walk with the Lord with gold, silver, and precious stones. And I knew this would take effort and time. It would require a sacrifice of putting God first in my life. For this reason, my days always start with prayer. Not a little prayer—often, it takes about three hours of prayer before I communicate with another person.

WATERFALLS FROM A ROCK

"He opened the rock, and the waters gushed out; They ran in the dry places like a river" (Psalm 105:41 KJV).

This remarkable experience also occurred during the community corporate prayer meetings. It happened in a morning worship service at the Voice of Praise Church in Bluewell, WV.

The choir was leading the congregation into a time of worship. My hands were raised, and I could feel the presence of the Lord moving in the church. Like the ocean waves that splash water over those close to the shore, the peace of God gushed upon me and the people.

Then I saw it—a huge rock, a heavenly rock, sitting upon the altar. From each side of the rock, heavenly water spurted forth. It was flowing on both sides of the church.

The water ran out the door and into the parking lot. This was one of the most visible scenes because the rock was so large, and the water flowed out with great force. It reminded me of the waters Ezekiel saw.

RIVERS OF HEALING

"And it shall come to pass, that everything that lives, which moves, wherever the rivers shall come, shall live: and there shall be a very great multitude of fish, because these waters shall come thither: for they shall be healed; and everything shall live whither the river comes" (Ezekiel 47:9 KJV).

FROM THE TEMPLE

The waters were flowing from the temple. It refreshed those who were weary from spiritual warfare. Ezekiel saw a man who had a line in his hand. He went in an eastward direction and measured a thousand cubits.

Ezekiel describes the water flowing at a level of the ankles. Then it reached up to the knees. Gradually, it rose to the waist. Eventually, it grew so deep that he had to swim (Ezekiel 47:3-6).

Ezekiel tells us that everywhere these waters flow, healing and life occur (Ezekiel 47:9).

SHATLEY SPRINGS

This heavenly scene with the rock and the waters also reminded me of a place we visited when I was a child. My dad delighted in telling us about the healing properties at Shatley Springs located at 407 Shatley Springs Rd, Crumbler, NC.

In addition to the healing waters, there is a famous restaurant that flourishes in the area. It offers fabulous country cooking, attracting travelers from many different states. People even bring empty jugs to fill with the spring water, and they often line up around the area, eagerly waiting for their turn.

HISTORY

History tells of a man named Martin Shatley. On a summer day in 1890, he stumbled upon these springs. He dipped his hands and face in the water. Just a few hours later, he realized he was healed of a crippling skin disease that had afflicted him for many years. The word spread, and many people visited these healing waters.

CHAPTER 3

PROPHECY PLUS PEOPLE

Did you know that prophecies from God bring light into dark places?

"We have also a more sure word of prophecy; whereunto you do well that you take heed, as light shines in a dark place, until the day dawns and the day star arises in your hearts" (2 Peter 1:19 KJV).

HE PROPHESIED IN OUR HOUSE!

The new pastor and his wife wanted to bless all the people in the congregation. So, they asked to visit each household. I was so excited when they were scheduled to come to our house.

At this point in my life, I had much to learn about prophecy. And it would not be until the COVID-19 years that I would really learn how to recognize a false prophet. But such a discussion is for later.

The pastor and his wife began with a prayer for our entire family. They prayed for God's protection and provision, as well as for our child.

The beautiful presence of the Lord filled the room as they prayed. Then, the pastor prophesied over us. I remember these words:

"You will have divine connections in your life."

"You will be like a well-oiled machine." (I understood this to be in matters of family and ministry.)

DIVINE CONNECTIONS DID HAPPEN!

Such connections brought me into the prayer movement with Women's Aglow, The Voice of Praise Church, WIN (Worldwide Intercessory Network) PRAYER, the 24-Hour Prayer Network of Capitol Hill Prayer Partners, and Night Watch meetings for our nation!

FROM THE WOMB

I am convinced that God protected me before I was born, and I have seen His hand of protection throughout my life. There were times when I lay close to death, but God brought someone to assist me. On several occasions, He protected me from car accidents. However, His intervention in my life was most evident when a charcoal fire went wrong. Within seconds, my ears and hands were burned, but I praise God for the quick action of my husband who grabbed the hose.

"You formed my innermost parts; You knit me (together) in my mother's womb" (Psalm 139:13 AMP).

"Your eyes have seen my unformed substance; And in Your book were all written The days that were appointed for me, When as yet there was not one of them (even taking shape)" (Psalm 139:16 AMP).

PEOPLE LESSONS

I learned about prayer from those closest to me, particularly my mother. From her, I gleaned many valuable lessons. Firstly, she is a very generous person, always reaching out to help the poor in various ways. Additionally, she is incredibly determined and resilient, always wearing a smile on her face regardless of the circumstances. Even in her 80s, she maintains a strong work ethic and never quits.

I learned about nature from my father who has gone on to be with the Lord. I happily recall many a trout fishing trip, where we basked in the glory of a sunlit stream. He tempted many a fish with his fly-fishing pole. I watched numerous fish jump out of the water to catch flies!

PRAYER LESSONS

I learned valuable lessons about prayer from my family members. I am the first child in the family. My sister followed just 18 months after me, and despite our different personalities, we both attended church every Sunday and Wednesday. While she developed the skill of playing the piano and loved being involved in church, I learned to play the guitar, and together, we performed at several church events.

My sister taught me to be actively involved, which led me to join other intercessors and pray for the nation. I even participated in prayer conference calls with people from different countries. My brother, who is 10 years younger than me, was also committed to the church. Both he and his wife taught young people, and to this day, they remain steadfast in their walk with God.

GET MARRIED: THE SPIRIT SAID

Kenny Hankla and I had dated for five years. He was a devoted Christian, and he remains committed to Christ. We loved each other deeply, but on the night before the wedding, I became afraid. Yes, afraid. I worried that I might not be able to be the kind of wife he needed, and I searched for more confidence.

As I pondered my future, a loud voice suddenly filled the room. I was the only one in the room. The voice spoke again, even louder. It said: "Marry Kenny! Marry Kenny!"

I sensed that the Holy Spirit did not want me to miss this important event. To this day, marrying Kenny has been one of the best decisions I have ever made!

AN ANGEL BY THE BABY

During my pregnancy, I spent many hours in the rocking chair of the baby's room. I would lay my hands on my stomach and pray for my child's health and well-being.

As birth approached, choosing a name for the baby became a top priority. I wanted a name that would please my in-laws and other relatives.

One day, as I was praying, the Holy Spirit placed the name Christopher Mark Hankla in my spirit. In Greek, the name Christopher means bearer or carrier of Christ and the biblical meaning of Mark is "shining."

This child would become a computer expert. He literally kept our church alive during the COVID-19 months. He set up online services on YouTube. Even to this day, we continue to reach out on that platform, allowing us to connect with more people. In addition, it has facilitated online giving, which has been vital.

BIRTH AND AN ANGEL

When the time came for me to give birth, a friend and an intercessor named Libby Repass stayed with us. Kenny and I appreciated her support during the birth of our child. I noticed that she was standing at the end of the bed, and was praying. Also, she appeared to see something. After the birth, I found out that she saw an angel in the room.

THE BREAKFAST PRAYER GROUP

This prayer group was very supportive of me as the mother of a young child. We prayed for our families, our children, our husbands, and their jobs.

On Saturday mornings, we ate breakfast together and prayed. We also shared scriptures and encouraged one another. Often, we walked along a beautiful country road and prayed as well.

We could feel the presence of God in these meetings and saw many answers to our prayers. Financial miracles happened. We prayed for the sick and witnessed people recover and for the schools and the churches.

Libby Repass, Tammy Kidd, and the pastor's wife were regular participants in this group!

> Again I say unto you, That if two of you shall agree on earth as touching any thing that they shall ask, it shall be done for them of my Father which is in heaven. For where two or three are gathered together in my name, there am I in the midst of them. (Matthew 18:19-20 KJV)

THE SUNSHINE PRAYER WARRIOR

"And whatsoever you shall ask in my name, that will I do, that the Father may be glorified in the Son. If you shall ask any thing in my name, I will do it" (John 14:13-14 KJV).

Our neighbors, Bill and Kaveda Reynolds, are unique prayer warriors. Kaveda can pray for sunshine any time of the year. I have called her frequently asking her to pray for some sun. In just a few hours, the dark clouds would leave, and the sun would shine through.

THE DAY THE DEVIL CAME TO THE PRAYER MEETING

As mentioned earlier, the home prayer meetings were very helpful for me as a young mother. Praying for families should be a high priority.

One day, a new person who was going through a difficult time came to the prayer meeting. She was invited by a member of the prayer team. She asked us to share scriptures and to pray for her. She listened to the scriptures with great interest and then, she invited us to pray for her.

As we prayed, her countenance changed. She squirmed in her chair and suddenly, her eyes rolled back in her head, and her face was twisted.

We prayed for peace and salvation in the name of Jesus. After about ten minutes, she returned to her normal self. Her eyes came back into the proper position, and her face relaxed. She left the meeting on a positive note, and I believe she was glad she came.

FACE-TO-FACE WITH A DEMON-OPPRESSED PERSON

I had another encounter with a demon-oppressed person, and believe me; these are not pleasant meetings. I had a scheduled meeting with her, but nobody else was allowed in the room. Looking back, that should have been a clue for me, and I should have insisted on having another person present.

My purpose for the meeting was to listen to the individual's complaint, but I did not expect the response I received. She lashed out at me with loud and ugly words and completely lost control. I had to take a few steps back to protect myself.

Then, her eyes rolled back inside her head, and her face became twisted and rigid. With a glazed look in her eyes, her body began jerking and moving back and forth.

HOSTILE ATMOSPHERE

The atmosphere in that room was hostile. The person was jerking so much that I thought I would get hit. I just sat still in silence, praying quietly and not making any sudden moves.

Then someone knocked on the door and noises were heard in the hall. Thank goodness, help was on the way! She must have heard the knock on the door because she quickly moved back from me. Her eyes rolled back to a normal position; the jerking motions stopped, and she looked toward the door before leaving the room.

I was alive and very thankful. God did not leave me alone; He sent someone to intervene.

HE REMINDED ME OF APOSTLE PAUL

Bishop Kenneth Kingrea

"Be you followers of me, even as I also am of Christ" (I Corinthians 11:1 KJV).

Bishop Kingrea was a man who followed Christ with all of his heart. He set a godly example for many people in the ministry, including me. I began the WIN Prayer Ministry for the Appalachian Conference under his leadership. He was truly a great mentor.

I was blessed to continue this ministry under Bishop Preston Mathena who also embraced prayer. I was surrounded by leaders who taught about prayer and who prayed.

Both Bishop Kingrea and his wife prayed over all the churches in the Appalachian Conference. At that time, about 160 churches and pastors needed prayer.

Bishop Kingrea had a great desire to see the churches thrive and to provide training for those in the ministry. He wanted every church to have a prayer ministry. This was part of my job to help churches develop prayer programs.

These scriptures from apostle Paul reveal the strong faith of Bishop Kingrea:

"Brethren, I count not myself to have apprehended: but this one thing I do, forgetting those things which are behind, and reaching forth unto those things which are before. I press toward the mark for the prize of the high calling of God in Christ Jesus" (Philippians 3:13-14 KJV).

WONDER WOMEN

These wonder women I refer to are part of the WIN prayer team. They are skilled prayer warriors! Like special forces in the military, these women embrace prayer assignments that relate to the following:

- Prayer for the United States—they have attended the National Day of Prayer events in Washington, D.C. for about 15 years.
- They pray in all-night prayer events for the nation.
- They pray with 24-hour prayer ministries.

Climbing to the top of famous mountain peaks to pray and blow the shofar is one type of prayer adventure.

Mount Mitchell is the highest peak of the Appalachian Mountains located in the Black Mountain Range.

I led a prayer meeting on a beautiful August day at the top of this mountain. There, prayer was made for the protection of the East Coast. The altitude was so high, we literally looked at the clouds below us as we prayed.

Pastor Debbie Hutton and Emily Perkins led a prayer team to a local mountaintop to pray for Southwest Virginia. They blew the shofar, worshiped God, and prayed for His protection upon our region and for revival.

Prayer walks during the National Day of Prayer were also conducted.

Pastor Debbie Hutton and Emily Perkins have stayed with me for over fifteen years. I can count on them to be there. They faithfully attend these prayer events for the nation and our region.

BOB EVANS – A PLACE OF DIVINE CONNECTIONS

A WIN prayer event was held in Pigeon Forge, Tennessee. Intercessors from several states attended. This inspiring event featured some famous prayer leaders and was life-changing for me. I became connected with intercessors who gave me daily prayer support. Every day, I could count on them to pray for me and my family.

How did this happen? During a lunch break, we were given about one hour to eat at the place of our choice. Bob Evans was closest to the hotel, and it was within walking distance.

Ron and Sandra Fowler, prayer leaders from South Carolina, spotted me when I entered. They invited me to eat with them. Immediately, we connected, and I enjoyed talking to them. We were able to discuss prayer topics, and we prayed about our concerns.

Six days a week, we pray with each other on the phone. Ron and Sandra have also been key speakers at our church and conferences on several occasions.

"A word in due season" was given to me on many occasions because of their prayers (Proverbs 15:23).

I have experienced numerous victories due to their prayers. Could it be that angels assisted with this divine connection?

"Again, I say unto you, That if two of you shall agree on earth as touching anything that they shall ask, it shall be done for them of My Father which is in heaven. For where two or three are gathered together in My name, there I am in the midst of them" (Matthew 18:19-20 KJV).

CHAPTER 4

SEVEN LAMPS
AND TWO OLIVE TREES

And the angel who was speaking with me came back and awakened me, like a man who is awakened out of his sleep. He said to me, 'What do you see?' I said, 'I see, and behold, a lampstand all of gold, with its bowl (for oil) on the top of it and its seven spouts belonging to each of the lamps which are on the top of it. And there are two olive trees by it, one on the right side of the bowl and the other on its left side (supplying it continuously with oil). (Zechariah 4:1-3 KJV)

This vision from the book of Zechariah inspired me to pursue the ministry.

A MOUNTAIN OF PROBLEMS

The vision provided encouragement for Zerubbabel and the nation. They had started to rebuild the temple, which was very important to the people. It served as a place of worship and unity. However, it would not be easy to build the temple as the Assyrians opposed its rebuilding. In addition, the people grew weary of the work that had started twenty years and would take another four years to complete.

The task of rebuilding the temple was very significant. God's light and glory from this temple would reach the nations of the world.

Zerubbabel needed supernatural assistance. Therefore, the angel woke him up and showed him the source of strength.

"Not by might, nor by power, but by My Spirit, says the Lord of hosts" (Zechariah 4:6).

God's message inspired Zerubbabel to continue. As they did Zerubbabel, these words encouraged me when I entered the ministry of prayer.

PASS THE BATON

Every word of this powerful message entered the depths of my spirit. The context came from the well-known scriptures of faith in Hebrews Chapter 11.

It was a beautiful summer evening at the conference center in Dublin, Virginia. Camp-meeting services were being conducted in the mornings and the evenings. People flooded to the altar after the message.

The main theme was "Passing the Baton of Faith", and the question was, "Who would accept the baton?"

For a long time, I wanted to enter the ministry to teach, pray, and help those in need. As I stood at the altar, I could sense the sovereign presence of God nudging me to do so.

THE QUESTION

A major obstacle stood between me and the ministry. I was a woman! I had never seen a woman preach or pastor in the churches in my region, even though I grew up in church and visited other churches in the area. The only roles women seemed to be assigned were playing the piano or teaching Sunday School. Could a woman be given an invitation to preach? Could a woman be voted as a pastor of a church?

A wave of disappointment came over me. Here I was at the altar, accepting the baton of ministry. Would I have any real opportunities to serve?

One thing helped me at that moment. I had faith in God's Word. I believed if He called me that He could place me in

His service.

FROM PRAYER TO PRAYER

The Voice of Praise Worship Center was a launching pad for ministry. Pastor Preston Mathena was a great supporter of prayer. He preached powerful messages about prayer. Kathy, his wife, was very involved in all aspects of ministry.

I attended the Wednesday night prayer meetings with a group of about eight regular attendees. We prayed for the church, our region, the schools, the sick, and other individual needs.

I looked forward to each meeting because God's presence could be felt during the services. His presence encouraged and strengthened me!

ALL-NIGHT PRAYER MEETINGS

As I stated, I went from prayer to prayer. I wondered if I could really pray all night. But the time went by so quickly.

McDOWELL COUNTY, WV

I recall the night when the team took a trip to a church in McDowell County. We were sent to pray for the churches in that area and for jobs to be created in the region. A map of the county was placed at the front of the church, listing the prayer needs for this church and others.

Although it was dark outside, God's light was shining brightly inside the church. This was my first corporate prayer meeting, and I quickly realized that in these gatherings, God's presence was very powerful. As the saying goes,

"Where you sow, you will reap." Years later, I became a pastor in this region and enjoyed a fruitful ministry

"A wicked person earns deceptive wages, but the one who sows righteousness reaps a sure reward" (Proverbs 11:18 KJV).

EVERY PLACE YOUR FEET SHALL TREAD, YOU WILL POSSESS

Prayer walking is a form of prayer that seeks to claim territory for the Lord. For example, a prayer team may walk around a church and pray for God's protection. A scripture that is often used for this type of prayer is found in the book of Joshua. After Moses died, Joshua became God's choice for the new leader.

The Lord encouraged Joshua by assuring him that the nation would be victorious in battle, and that every place the people's feet walked upon, they would possess.

"Every place that the sole of your foot shall tread upon, that have I given unto you, as I said unto Moses" (Joshua 1:3 KJV).

THE FUTURE CHURCH IN TAZEWELL, VIRGINIA

At another all-night prayer meeting, the team was sent to pray over a plot of land. The prayer leader was a godly man who loved God and set an excellent example of Christian character. He was also skilled in leading corporate prayer.

Our task was to pray for a new church to be planted on that land. So, the prayer leader put oil on the shoes of all the participants. Then he led us around the land. We circled the plot several times and prayed for a church to be established.

All night, we prayed for this church. We prayed for the finances to build the church, for future leaders of the church, and for the people of this region to be drawn to the church.

In a few years, we saw the fruit of our labor. A church called Destiny was built and its members reached out to the community. It is a flourishing church and thrives even today.

THE VISION SEEN DURING ORDINATION

Finally, the day arrived for me to become an ordained minister. Now, I could explore job opportunities such as pastoring a church and working in hospices. Also, I could officially perform marriage ceremonies and funerals.

I completed all classes and requirements for this event. The ordination ceremony was held at the Appalachian Conference Center in Dublin, Virginia.

It was the custom of the conference leaders to pray for the candidates and their families. Several people were ahead of me, so I waited patiently.

Finally, we were called to come to the front for prayer. We sat in chairs and bowed our heads in reverence to God. The leaders prayed over us and blessed our families. Suddenly, one leader saw a vision regarding our future ministry.

THE VISION

The vision included scripture references from Zechariah Chapter 4. One of the leaders saw the heavenly menorah over our family. God's light was shining on us! Now, those heavenly lamps and olive trees took on a personal meaning.

As they prayed, God's presence swept over me. I could hear the words that brought Zerubbabel so much encouragement.

"Then he answered and spoke to me, saying, 'This is the Word of the LORD unto Zerubbabel, Not by might, nor by power, but by my spirit,' says the LORD of hosts" (Zechariah 4:6 KJV).

72

God's light shone within my heart and on my path.

THE CHURCH IN COAL COUNTRY

The Big Four P. H. Church is located in Kimball, WV. The church needed someone to fill in and conduct Sunday morning services.

The conference called to see if I would be interested. Even though the church was about an hour's drive from our house, we decided to go.

I fell in love with the church and its people. They were very appreciative of all our efforts, and a divine connection between the Big Four Church and our family developed over time. We looked forward to going to church every Sunday because the leaders offered us strong support. Even more importantly, they were strong intercessors.

TIME TO VOTE

Even though I felt that I would be voted as the pastor, it was a great feeling when it became official. Conference leaders were there to oversee the ceremony, and a fellowship meal concluded the service

SCRIPTURE CONFIRMATION

I learned early in my ministry to ask God for scripture confirmation for every event. Again, my prayer was, "Let me see what You are saying."

I saw mountains and valleys. I saw mountain streams rushing from the mountain sides. I saw sunlight along the road to the church.

Then, a scripture arose in my spirit that led me Sunday after Sunday to the Big Four P.H. Church.

"For you shall go out with joy, and be led forth with peace: the mountains and the hills shall break forth before you into singing, and all the trees of the field shall clap their hands" (Isaiah 55:12 KJV).

GO OUT INTO THE HIGHWAYS AND HEDGES

Jesus told a parable of a certain man who prepared a great supper and invited many people to come. He summoned his servants to go to the invited guests and remind them of the supper. However, one after another made excuses not to come.

One guest said he had bought a plot of land and needed to go and inspect it. Therefore, he could not come. Another said he had bought five yokes of oxen and had to go and claim them. For this reason, he could not come. Another told the servants that he had just gotten married and could not attend.

The great man who prepared the supper was angry because the people would not accept his invitation. So, he told his servants to go and invite others.

That servant came and showed his lord these things. Then the master of the house being angry said to his servants,

> Go out quickly into the streets and lanes of the city, and bring in hither the poor, and the maimed, and the halt (those who could not walk), and the blind. And the servant said, Lord, it is done as you have commanded, and

yet there is room. And the Lord said unto the servant, Go out into the highways and hedges, and compel them to come in, that my house may be filled. (Luke 14:21-23 KJV)

"Compel" is a strong action word. It implies using force or pressure.

We had to make strong efforts to encourage people to attend church, as is the case for many other small American churches in rural areas. Despite this struggle, we were able to find a few people who remained faithful to God and the church.

COMPEL THEM TO COME

One of the first things we did to encourage people to come was to offer a spaghetti meal. People were interested, and several signed the attendance sheet. The event was held on a cold, windy day in March, and strong winds had knocked out power to several towns. Despite the weather conditions, we could not cancel the meal as this was our first outreach event!

My husband was wise enough to bring his camping equipment just in case, and this turned out to be a good decision. Additionally, an elder of the church provided assistance. When we arrived at the church, several people had already come, but there was no electricity. However, this did not stop us from serving the meal. My husband used his camping stove to cook a spaghetti meal, and there was enough food for everyone.

Overall, serving meals proved to be a great way to reach out to the community.

INVITE A FRIEND

Prayer was a vital part of our efforts to encourage people to come. We prayed for our friends, family members, and the community. Additionally, members of the church reached out to their friends and family, and we saw some new people attend. We found that there is power in a personal invitation.

TEEN CHALLENGE

A group of young people traveled from church to church, testifying about how God had delivered them from drugs and other negative lifestyles. This group visited our church several times, and their testimonies drew new people to our services. As a result of this ministry, one person desired to be baptized. The baptism was conducted on the bank of a local river.

BAPTISM ON THE BEACH

Hungry Mother State Park in Virginia has a beautiful lake and beach. It is a favorite vacation escape for those who like to camp, fish, or hike. The lake and the mountains create a peaceful atmosphere.

One afternoon on August 14th, 2022, Jeff was baptized at this park. He joined the church with the online services during the COVID-19 shutdowns.

Faithfully, he listened to the Sunday YouTube services and gave offerings via the online giving link. He also attempted to attend church on-site once a month. To do so, he had to travel about two hours.

READY

Jeff was ready to be baptized. In addition to being faithful to join the online services, he was eager to experience the blessings of baptism.

At the campsite, I read scriptures about baptism and prayed for Jeff. He confirmed that he had indeed prayed for Jesus to be his Lord and Savior, had repented of his sins, and had chosen to follow Christ.

AT THE BEACH

A few people celebrated this event with Jeff. My husband and son walked with us to find a quiet place on the beach. I conducted the ceremony, and my husband assisted with dunking Jeff in the water. My son provided music for the occasion.

As Jeff emerged from the water, a lady sitting on a towel clapped. She raised her hands and praised the Lord. She was so excited for him!

"Go you therefore, and teach all nations, baptizing them in the name of the Father, and of the Son, and of the Holy Ghost" (Matthew 28:19 KJV).

THE TEN-THOUSAND-DOLLAR MIRACLE

After several years, the Big Four P.H. Church needed some major repairs.

Money and manpower were necessary. Two major floods brought devastation to parts of the county and also damaged the basement floor of the church. The basement of the church had to be remodeled and the women's bathroom needed new walls. Other areas also needed repairs.

The insurance company told us they would drop our coverage if we did not repair the church. My husband and a few others were able to repair some areas, but there was so much more to be done.

WHO WOULD HELP?

I prayed much about these needs. In faith, I called for divine connections. Finally, one day, we received a call from the Conference Missions Department. Larry Meadors, the director, was the heavenly link.

He had received a call from a church in South Carolina that went on mission trips every year. They frequently traveled to other countries, but this year, they could not go overseas because of COVID-19 restrictions. Therefore, they wanted to help a church in the rural areas of West Virginia.

The rest of the story is history. There was a divine connection of light.

The people from this church in South Carolina were amazing. Both young and old people worked on the Big Four Church. They painted it and made one repair after another. A new women's bathroom was built. They spent around ten thousand dollars fixing the church. And they were skilled in remodeling.

BUILD THE OLD WASTE PLACES

Several years ago, I attended a prayer conference in South Carolina. The speaker was a well-known prayer leader in our organization. She had the gift of praying for people and prophesying. She is a true woman of God, with an anointing for prayer. Her desire was to build a 24-hour prayer center.

She looked in my direction, and I heard these words from the book of Isaiah.

"And your people will rebuild the ancient ruins; You will raise up and restore the age-old foundations (of buildings that have been laid waste); You will be called Repairer of the Breach, Restorer of Streets with Dwellings" (Isaiah 58:12 AMP).

I knew this scripture well and that the promise is for those who provide aid to the poor and helpless. It applied to me. I could sense that at some point in the future, I would be involved in a rebuilding process.

COAL COUNTRY

The Big Four P.H. Church is named after four famous coal mining companies that flourished about 70 years ago. An old picture is hanging on the wall of the church. In this picture is a group of about eighty people who were members of the church during this prosperous time.

Coal mining declined significantly with the growth of new energy sources. McDowell County was once flourishing. Now it struggles to provide jobs and lacks financial stability. Many families have moved out of the area to find employment. Several dilapidated buildings occupy the county and sit along the highways!

NEHEMIAH FROM SOUTH CAROLINA

The book of Nehemiah is inspirational for pastors who find themselves in the process of rebuilding. In just 52 days, Nehemiah rebuilt the city walls of Jerusalem. He gathered the people for this task and equipped them. Nothing would stop him. Even when threatened by enemies, he continued to build.

The Big Four P.H. Church needed someone like Nehemiah. Dawn Morris from the Hickory Grove IPHC Church in South Carolina was that person. Her husband Brad was very supportive and had a gift of generosity. Dawn was gifted to assess the situation and assign the right people to the job. She had the vision to see God's churches restored and revived. Dawn and her husband brought a team of remarkable people to the Big Four P.H. Church. Many of them had taken vacation time to be with us. Other members of the team were older, being in their 70s and even 80s. Yet, they worked long days.

IN JUST ONE WEEK

It was amazing to see projects performed quickly and with excellence. Bathrooms were rebuilt. The walls were repaired. The old kitchen was replaced with a new one. Both the inside and outside of the church received fresh paint. And new curtains and windows appeared. By the end of the week, the Big Four P.H. Church looked new.

This team committed to returning. They wanted to do more!

In a county of old waste places, the Big Four P.H. Church shined!

FEED MY SHEEP

The Big Four P.H. Church received other miracles in addition to the ones mentioned earlier. The holiday season in the county can be a difficult time for many families who struggle to put enough food on the table for a Christmas meal. The church felt a strong desire to reach out to the community and bring hope during the holidays, but there was not enough funding for this mission.

Once again, the church turned to prayer and asked for divine connections and guidance. The scriptures that inspired the church in this direction are found in the story of Jesus appearing to Peter and some of the other disciples after His resurrection. During this encounter, Jesus had a fire of coals burning and provided a meal of fish and bread, and they dined together on the beach. It was during this meal that Jesus gave Peter some important instructions.

"So, when they had dined, Jesus said to Simon Peter, 'Simon, son of Jonas, lovest thou Me more than these?' He said unto him, 'Yea, Lord; you know that I love you.' He said, 'Feed my Lambs'" (John 21:15 KJV).

In a second and third conversation, Jesus told Peter, "Feed my sheep."

EYES THAT SEE! HEARTS THAT HEAR!

Pastors Todd and Tammy Porter had already been inspired by the Holy Spirit to provide a food outreach for McDowell County. They were sensitive to the Holy Spirit, and their hearts were opened to the needs of the people.

They provided over sixty quality food baskets to the church and community. In addition, they assisted in the delivery of the food. Many of the families received prayer, along with food baskets.

CHAPTER 5

EARS FROM HEAVEN

The National Day of Prayer is observed every year on the first Thursday in May. Harry S. Truman established this event in 1952. President Ronald Regan moved the observance of this event to the first Thursday in May. However, its history goes back further. The First Continental Congress proclaimed several days of prayer and fasting in the year 1775.

George Washington, John Adams, and Abraham Lincoln all declared a day of prayer and fasting for the nation. Each year, the president is required by law to sign a proclamation to encourage all Americans to pray for the country.

Prayer groups from all fifty states come to pray at the Capitol on the National Day of Prayer.

SHE SAW THE HEAVENLY EAR

On one National Day of Prayer, our team from the Appalachian Conference was invited to lead a prayer session in Washington, D.C.

Johanna suddenly became very quiet while kneeling in prayer. I could tell that she was seeing something in the Spirit.

As I approached her, I began to see also. There was a very large ear from heaven turned toward the Capitol. Clouds surrounded the ear and light shined through the clouds. The ear was a living thing engaged in the job of hearing prayers. Light shined brightly during the entire episode.

"Let my prayer come before You and enter into Your presence. Incline Your ear to my cry!" (Psalm 88:2 AMP).

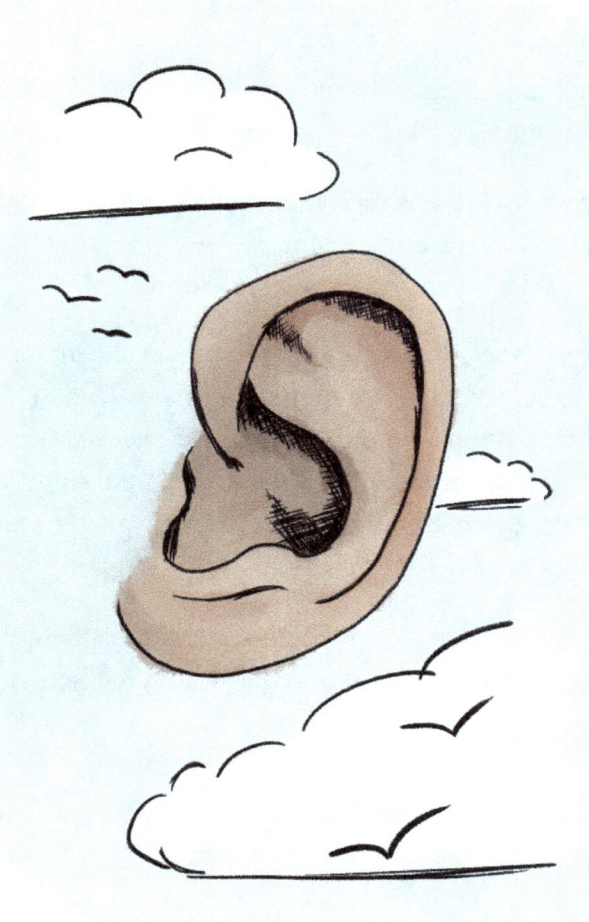

THE ANGEL OVER THE PENTAGON

The Appalachian Conference Prayer Team received resources and prayer support from Bishop Preston Mathena, Ron Fredericks, Larry Meadors, and the Conference Board to attend these events.

The team took great measures to prepare for this day. About eight weeks before the event, weekly prayer calls were conducted. Also, times of fasting were observed.

When we prayed in the corporate prayer meetings for the nation, we sensed the sovereign presence of God. The supernatural interventions were easy to notice. People were drawn to pray for each other. Intercessors declared significant scriptures over the nation. Others performed prayer walks around buildings to pray for protection.

In the corporate prayer meetings, the atmosphere was electrifying. It was charged with energy. Intercessors were united in the prayer focus.

THE PICTURE

During one of the early trips to The National Day of Prayer, we took lots of pictures. As we toured the area surrounding the Pentagon, I sensed a need to stop and wait.

During "the waiting," my son took several pictures of the Pentagon. After a while, we continued on our tour of Washington, D.C.

When we returned home, we sent the pictures to be developed. Finally, we were able to see them. They reflected precious memories, but there was something else. In one of the pictures, a large angel was over the Pentagon. His wings were spread wide, and he was looking directly over the Pentagon.

FLASHING LIGHTS OF RED, WHITE, AND BLUE

During another National Day of Prayer event, I saw an unusual display of lights as I was praying for the nation. Often, my prayers included protection for our leaders and wisdom.

With my physical eyes closed and my spiritual eyes opened, I sensed the Holy Spirit was allowing me to see this heavenly scene, so I could pray more effectively.

This was no small display of lights. The lights extended beyond the room. In a cadence, they flashed colors of red, white, and blue for about ten minutes.

It was not a warning type of display, but rather, a message of confirmation that our prayers were being heard in heaven. Our prayers seemed to have ascended to heaven in the form of colors.

They were prayed in faith, and decrees were made directly from God's Word, which does not return to Him void.

"So shall my word be that goes forth out of my mouth; it shall not return unto me void, but it shall accomplish that which I please, and it shall prosper in the thing whereto I sent it" (Isaiah 55:11 KJV).

BEFORE GOD'S THRONE

Light flashes around God's throne and sounds of thunder are heard.

"From the throne came flashes of lightning and (rumbling) sounds and peals of thunder. Seven lamps of fire were burning in front of the throne, which are the seven Spirits of God" (Revelation 4:5 AMP).

SARA REMINDED ME OF DEBORAH

Deborah was a judge in the nation of Israel. She stood firm in the face of battle. When Jabin, the king of Canaan, sent Sisera his captain to wage war against Israel, Deborah arose on the scene (Judges Chapter 4).

Deborah was also an encourager. She encouraged Israel's captain, Barak, not to fear this enemy. He was afraid because Sisera had nine hundred chariots of iron.

Barak told Deborah he would only go to battle if she went with him. Without hesitation, Deborah displayed great courage and accompanied him.

It was a supernatural victory. Scripture tells us that God discomfited Sisera, and all of his chariots (Judges 4:15).

PRESIDENT OF CAPITOL HILL PRAYER PARTNERS

Sara Ballenger is the president of this organization that participates in the National Day of Prayer events. She is the one who extended invitations to the Appalachian Prayer Team to come and join in the prayer activities for the nation.

Sara's sense of humor relaxed our team, and we enjoyed special fellowship times dining at the Mexican restaurant.

Like Deborah, Sara has strong faith and is an encourager. She leads 24-hour prayer, all-night prayer, and many other prayer events.

Deloris Purvis is also from the Appalachian Conference and a participant in the National Day of Prayer events. She stands firmly by Sara's side and holds up her arms in prayer. Deloris is a woman of wisdom, faith, and prophetic giftings.

WHY SHOULD WE PRAY FOR OUR NATION?

Praying for the nation's leaders is pleasing in God's sight. Let us not forget that heaven looks upon us. Our actions are noted, not only on the earth but also in heaven.

Three reasons to pray for the nation's leaders are noted in the following scripture:

> I exhort therefore, that, first of all, supplications, prayers, intercessions, and giving of thanks, be made for all men. For kings, and for all that are in authority; that we may lead a quiet and peaceable (peaceful) life in all godliness and honesty. For this is good and acceptable in the sight of God our Savior: Who will have all men to be saved, and to come unto the knowledge of the truth. (1 Timothy 2:1-4 KJV)

REASON ONE

Scriptures exhort or urge us to pray. "Urge" is a strong word. Prayers for kings and all in authority can bring positive changes to the nation. Can we expect anything good to happen if we don't pray?

Most leaders ask for prayers. They have to make decisions that affect large numbers of people. Like King Solomon, many leaders desire wisdom to do what is right for the nation.

REASON TWO

We are told that we can live quiet and peaceful lives in all godliness and honesty. Quiet refers to the fact that we will not be troubled from without, and peace suggests that we will not be troubled from within.

REASON THREE

These prayers are good and acceptable in the sight of God. The mere fact that we can please God is sufficient reason to pray for the leaders of the nation.

SHIPS ON THE SEA

At another National Day of Prayer event, other heavenly scenes were revealed. A group of about thirty intercessors was praying in **a room** in Washington, D.C.

We were divided into groups and given prayer assignments. Prayers were offered for various areas of the government. Protection for our nation was also a major prayer focus.

I was praying with a group of people when suddenly, a heavenly scene appeared. Ships were on the sea that seemed to be from the U.S. Navy. They were sitting on the sea, just waiting.

There was a sense of a possible conflict with an enemy ship or submarine. Even though the ships were sitting still, there was an atmosphere of preparation for hostile action.

I was not the only one who saw the ships and recognized them as part of the Navy. Several other intercessors saw them.

So, our prayer focus was directed toward the Navy. We prayed for protection and the ability to detect any hostile events. We also prayed for the leaders to be given wisdom.

God's presence permeated the room.

DO NOT NEGLECT TO PRAY FOR OUR LEADERS

Make a plan to pray at least once a week for the leaders of the nation. Remember this is pleasing in God's sight.

The prophet Samuel prayed for King Saul and took it seriously.

"Moreover, as for me, far be it from me that I should sin against the Lord by ceasing to pray for you; but I will instruct you in the good and right way" (1 Samuel 12:23 AMP).

CHAPTER 6

MONEY COME!

I met a woman who was elderly but very active. She came to the exercise class that I taught for seniors. I knew she was a Christian, but I did not know much about her prayer life.

One day, I closed my door and sought privacy. I had a stack of charts to complete. Suddenly, I heard a knock on the door. It was her! She rushed into my office when I opened the door, sat in an empty chair, and said: "I came to pray for you."

I told her I did not have time to pray and to wait until tomorrow. She was not angry but jumped from her chair and went out the door.

When she left my office, I sensed the presence of the Holy Spirit. He had a message for me, and I chose to listen. He said, "If you do not have time to pray, you do not have time for Me!"

Quickly, I ran down the hall and found her. I said, "Irene, come back. Let's pray!"

She prayed for me, and for money to come to meet my needs. She prayed for money to come in the right way, God's way, and for financial resources to be released to me.

I did not know that one could pray for money to come.

IT HAPPENED

Over the course of the week, money came to me by checks in the mail and refunds. I saw God do a makeover in our finances. I saw bills get paid and debts canceled. The financial pressure began to ease when I saw God bring money by His ways.

My grandfather was a very good businessman. He was a farmer and knew how to make a profit. Often, he told me, "Money does not grow on trees."

My sister and I worked on the farm with him. We helped with the sheep and the cows and cut thistles from the ground. My grandfather made sure that we were rewarded.

It was news to me that we can pray for money to come. But then I was reminded about the prophet Elijah.

THE BROOK

There was a judgment of drought upon the land, but Elijah would not be affected by this judgment. He would not suffer from lack. God had a plan and a place of provision for Elijah. God told him to go to the brook Cherith. At this brook, he received fresh water. God commanded ravens to bring him food every morning and evening.

"And the ravens brought him bread and flesh in the morning, and bread and flesh in the evening, and he drank of the brook" (1 Kings 17:6 KJV).

The Lord's Prayer also tells us to pray for our daily bread. Our Father is concerned about our daily needs (Matthew 6:11).

BREAK THE BRASS GATES AND THE IRON BARS

When we were first married, my husband was in search of a particular job. When he saw a vacancy for it, he applied. However, we did not hear back from the company. So, I sought the Lord on how to pray for this situation. The scripture about the gates of brass and the bars of iron came to my attention.

"Oh, that men would praise the Lord for his goodness, and for his wonderful works to the children of men! For he has broken the gates of brass, and cut the bars of iron in sunder" (Psalm 107:15, 16 KJV).

I opened the Bible to these scriptures. Day after day, I prayed these very words.

I prayed that all hindrances would be removed and for the door to be open for my husband. Within a short time, he got the call to come. He was hired and worked in a job he loved for many years. He also made life-long friendships.

LAID OFF

For nearly fourteen years, I worked as an exercise physiologist at a wellness center. I enjoyed my work, and I loved the job because I saw many people improve their health. But one day, over 300 people were laid off from the hospital that sponsored the wellness center. Hence, it was shut down. This was a disappointment to many people in the area, including me. I needed another job, so I sought the Lord on how to pray for it.

I sensed that the Holy Spirit wanted me to wait in silence every morning for forty minutes with an attitude of faith.

A scripture came to my mind, which confirmed these instructions.

"From the days of old no one has heard, nor has ear perceived, Nor has the eye seen a God besides You, Who works and acts in behalf of the one who (gladly) waits for Him" (Isaiah 64:4, 5 AMP).

Within a month, I received a job at another wellness center where I was close to my family and friends. It was a good situation, and I loved the work.

THE TWENTY-DOLLAR RESCUE

I understood the concept of planting a seed and receiving a harvest. Being raised on the farm, we planted lots of seeds, including strawberries, squash, beans, and corn. Also, we enjoyed the time of harvest. The food from the garden was delicious.

One scripture tells us what we sow, we will reap.

"Be not deceived; God is not mocked: for whatsoever a man sows, that shall he also reap" (Galatians 6:7 KJV).

I made it a practice to give twenty dollars each month to a ministry that taught me truths from God's Word. I prayed over the offering and asked for a harvest in return. By harvest, I expected things such as favor, protection, and peace.

It seemed like a small offering, but I was giving from my

heart.

"Every man according as he purposes in his heart, so let him give; not grudgingly, or of necessity, for God loves a cheerful giver" (2 Corinthians 9:7 KJV).

BLACK ICE

When I worked with cardiac rehabilitation, I had to be on the job at 6:00 a.m. I liked these hours because we got off early. However, I had to drive about 30 miles very early in the morning.

One morning, I forgot to check the weather or travel information. Down the interstate I went, zipping along at about sixty-five miles an hour. Normally, this speed would be fine, but not this morning! I noticed that cars were moving slowly.

Then I saw it. Black ice! It was too late for me to slow down. My car crossed a bridge and landed high up in the ditch.

NOT A SCRATCH! NOT A BRUISE!

When the car finally came to a halt, it was sitting on a soft bank that was high off the ground.

I did not hit another car!

I did not go off the bridge!

I did not cross the median!

It was as if an angel intervened and steered my car away from danger.

I checked myself. I was breathing. I had no pain. I saw no blood! When help arrived, I was not harmed. The people who assisted me seemed very surprised that I was doing well.

I ASKED GOD

For a few minutes, I was left alone. During that time, I asked God a very important question, and the answer would inspire me to be a giver in God's kingdom.

I asked God, "Why was I not hurt?" Of course, I was glad. Yet, I was curious how I escaped such great danger.

THEN I HEARD! AND I SAW!

The Holy Spirit brought to my attention that just a few days ago, I had given a $20 offering. Like a replay on television, I saw myself giving the offering.

"This offering saved your life. You reaped the harvest of protection."

God's Word promises those who tithe that He will rebuke the devourer (Malachi 3:11). In addition to giving offerings, I was a tither! Neither my life nor my car was devoured.

MY FIRST NEW CAR

Our family was fortunate to have received some secondhand cars that had already been driven several miles. However, we struggled in the area of cars. Almost every car we drove needed its oil replaced at least once a week, and most of them had check engine lights that stayed on. We took the cars to be inspected to find out the cause of the check engine light, and most of the time we were told that it was the catalytic converter. Unfortunately, this part cost over two hundred dollars!

Finally, I realized that if I were to ever own a new car, I would have to pray for it.

THE TITLE DEED

I prayed about the new car and asked the Father to show me a scripture I could claim with faith. I knew that without faith it is impossible to please God (Hebrews 11:6).

"Now faith is the assurance (title deed, confirmation) of things hoped for (divinely guaranteed), and the evidence of things not seen (the conviction of their reality-faith comprehends as fact what cannot be experienced by the physical senses.)" (Hebrews 11:1 AMP).

When I prayed this scripture, I saw (in the spirit) a title deed to a car. I also received instructions from the Holy Spirit.

I usually walked two to three miles a day several times a week. There was a car lot with new cars just a mile from my house. Day after day, I walked to this car lot and prayed. I walked around the new cars and prayed about owning the title deed to a new car.

A MAZDA 323

In addition to praying over the cars, I saved money. It seemed as if God's Spirit helped me to save. Each month, I was able to put money into a special "car fund."

The day finally came when I sat down with a car dealer and negotiated for a maroon Mazda 323. Maybe, you can remember this model. It was highly rated and had plenty of room for us. But while signing the papers, the dealer said I did not have enough credit to buy the car. I did not have any bad credit. However, I was young and did not have enough time to build up credit. Despite this setback, I did not give up. I told the dealer that I had $6000 ready to pay for it. That was about two-thirds of the cost of the car.

Suddenly, he forgot all about the credit and sold me the car. That was a great vehicle. It was reliable and did not need many repairs.

Over 270,000 miles were put on that car, and it was still running. At that point, Kenny's dad really needed a car. So, we gave it to him. It served him well.

A BRICK HOUSE

I had always wanted a brick house. It reminded me of the story that Jesus told about the house built upon a rock.

"Therefore whosoever hears these sayings of mine, and does

them, I will liken him unto a wise man, which built his house upon a rock: and the rain descended, and the floods came, and the winds blew, and beat upon that house; and it fell not: for it was founded upon a rock" (Matthew 7:24-25 KJV).

My husband and I were both taught to tithe and give unto God's work. We did so and had frequent financial miracles. We were able to make double monthly payments several times.

Today, as I enjoy our house, I remember God's goodness!

"The blessing of the Lord, it makes rich, and adds no sorrow with it" (Proverbs 10:22 KJV).

BONUSES AND RAISES

At times, it was difficult to tithe. But we knew the great value of investing in God's kingdom. Our records show our commitment to this area. Both heaven and earth can search through the checkbooks and bank accounts and confirm this. God honored His Word. He said that we should try and prove Him in the area of tithes.

He says, "Prove me now herewith, says the Lord of hosts, if I will not open you the windows of heaven, and pour you out a blessing, that there shall not be room enough to receive it" (Malachi 3:10 KJV).

As we look back over the past, we see numerous times that my husband received bonuses and raises. And for this, we give thanks.

ALASKA, HERE WE COME!

All of my life, I have wanted to go to Alaska. I read books and watched television shows about it and longed to see the mountains, streams, and wildlife.

Our family began to pray about this trip because we knew it would take a miracle to get to Alaska. I looked for scriptures to pray, and I needed to see God's hand in this request. This trip started with God's Word.

"Delight yourself in the Lord; and he shall give you the desires of your heart" (Psalm 37:4 KJV).

LITTLE BY LITTLE

Our son found miracles. He had been searching for prices for cruises. He received an offer for $100 per person, for a 3-day cruise to other countries. But somehow it glitched and allowed us to apply this offer on a 10-day cruise to Alaska. This was truly a financial miracle!

We received another miracle with the costs of the airplane tickets, which was $300 a person for these flights to Alaska. We took advantage of this price and bought the tickets. Airplane prices steadily rose after our purchases.

One month before the flights, the cost rose to $1,600 a person. We saved $1,200 per person!

MOUNTAINS SPEAK

Mountains remind me of God's faithfulness and stability. During the cruise, I spent a lot of time just gazing upon the majestic sights of the Alaskan mountains.

My spiritual eyes were also opened on this trip. The very cover of this book was inspired by that trip. The light shining upon the waterfall speaks of God's life. Jesus told us He wants us to have life more abundantly!

"The thief comes only in order to steal and kill and destroy. I came that they may have and enjoy life, and have it in abundance (to the full, till it overflows) (John 10:10 AMP).

The mountains, streams, and hillsides of Alaska are much more beautiful than what we see on television.

OTHER SIGHTS

We enjoyed some time in Juneau, a city inaccessible by road. Yes, people have to fly or cruise into Juneau. Here we saw several eagles. Some were flying, while others were resting in trees.

A great surprise awaited us as we traveled to the Mendenhall Glacier. This site is also in Juneau, and we hiked about a mile to see it. Nature was on great display for us as we viewed the glacier!

Another highlight was a train ride into Canada. The landscape was amazing, and people were constantly taking pictures of the scenery. We passed Mounty Station in Canada and saw about two feet of snow in the month of May.

LOOK UNTO THE HILLS

I summarize the trip to Alaska with a favorite scripture:

"I will lift up my eyes to the hills—From where shall my help come? My help comes from the Lord" (Psalm 121:1, 2 AMP).

CHAPTER 7

PETS AND PRAYER

How can pets have any effect on a person's prayer life? The answer to this question depends upon the intercessor.

I had a cat named Snowflake. During my early morning prayer times, I found that I was not alone. She would come and sit next to me whenever she heard me start to pray. Frequently, she stayed for the entire prayer session, which generally lasted from two to three hours. The length of time depended upon the number of prayer requests.

Snowflake brought great comfort to our family. When my son came to visit, she expected to be petted. She would curl up next to him and purr. She loved to sit on the bed and look out the window.

During family prayer time, Snowflake would take her place beside us. She wanted to be around "praying people." Every now and then, she would meow during these times of prayer.

When my husband worked from home, as soon as he went to the computer, Snowflake would sit in a chair next to him.

There is a scripture that instructs us to care for our animals: "A righteous man regards the life of his beast: but the tender mercies of the wicked are cruel" (Proverbs 12:10 KJV).

PET THERAPY

Pets are brought to hospitals and nursing homes to cheer to the patients. Often, a patient will pet the dog, and talk to it. Love is expressed, and love is given!

Pets provide companionship. They amuse us and return love. They even protect us.

Our friend Jeff has a service dog named Max. This dog is loyal and supportive and even accompanied him to his baptism.

PETS THAT WENT TO CHURCH

I remember the first time Jeff came to the Big Four P. H. Church. He brought his service dog, Max, and he sat in the pew beside him. During the service, the dog lifted his head and listened to the message. Max also smiled at people around him and wagged his tail. They could not resist petting him.

Jeff said he had been looking for a church he could attend and bring his service dog. Max was welcome at the Big Four P.H. Church.

How many more people would attend church if they felt comfortable bringing their service dogs?

One of my friends was a wonderful Methodist minister who was fond of cats. She cared for the people and taught God's Word.

She told me that every few months the church would have a

pet service where people could bring their pets. She said this service attracted large crowds. At the end of the service, she prayed for the pets.

THE PET LAMB

During his warning to King David, a story of a pet lamb was told by Nathan the prophet. This story was told to open David's eyes, so he could see his sins regarding Bathsheba and her husband.

He talked about two men in a city. One man was rich and the other poor.

"The poor man had nothing, save one little ewe lamb, which he had bought and nourished up: and it grew up together with him, and with his children; and it did eat of his own meat, and drank of his own cup, and lay in his bosom, and was unto him as a daughter" (Samuel 12:3 KJV).

This lamb brought joy to the family.

BALAAM'S DONKEY

This narrative from Numbers Chapter 2, certainly describes how a pet should not be treated.

Balaam was also known to be a false prophet. He was hired by the king of Moab to place a curse upon the Israelites. Being concerned about this assignment, Balaam sought the Lord. He was instructed not to curse God's people. Nevertheless, Balak continued to urge Balaam to curse the Israelites.

One morning, Balaam prepared his donkey and headed toward the princes of Moab. God was very angry with Balaam because he went on this trip.

The Lord intervened to protect His people. The angel of the Lord, with his sword raised, stood in the path of the donkey. The donkey feared the angel and veered from the path. She ran Balaam into a field. In his anger, Balaam struck the donkey. They got back onto the path.

Again, the donkey saw the angel of the Lord and was frightened. To avoid the angel of the Lord, the donkey ran into the wall. Balaam's foot was compressed against the wall. Frustrated, he struck the donkey, another time.

Back on the path, the donkey saw that the angel of the Lord had moved further down the road. The pathway became very narrow, and the donkey could not turn to either side. She fell down with Balaam on her back. This time, Balaam was very angry. He had not seen the angel of the Lord, so he did not understand why the donkey was behaving as it did.

DONKEY TALK

The Lord opened the mouth of the donkey, and she asked what she had done to deserve the beatings. Balaam argued with the donkey. He even threatened that if he had a sword, he would kill her.

OPEN EYES

The Lord opened Balaam's eyes so he could also see the angel of the Lord with his sword raised. The angel then addressed Balaam and asked why he had beaten his donkey three times. Beating the donkey got the attention of the angel.

Balaam was able to see his sin. Hence, he bowed his face to the ground and repented.

LESSONS LEARNED

The main focus of this story is that God's people are not to be cursed. However, the treatment of animals is also addressed. Beating the donkey was unacceptable to the Lord. We can conclude that illtreating other animals is also unacceptable to Him.

A BUDDY CAME

Because of COVID-19 restrictions in his workplace, my husband, Kenny, was now working from home. Our son helped him install the computer and internet for his work. I helped prepare a room for an office.

My husband looked out the window as he worked. The window was located just a couple of feet above the porch. He had a good view of the mountains and my bird feeder.

One day, a young gray cat came to the window. It obviously did not have an owner. The cat sat in the window for hours and watched Kenny, and the two became attached.

Kenny built the cat a little house and put it on the porch. He liked the cat house but longed to be in the big house. We felt it was not really safe for him to be outside since he was so young.

Preparations were made for the cat to stay in the house. Quickly, he bonded with Kenny and followed him around the house and everywhere. He lay on Kenny's bed and sat with him in his TV chair and watched television.

We decided to name him Buddy when Kenny planned a trip to the vet. It was the best name we could give because indeed, the two were buddies!

A GIFT JUST IN TIME

We did not realize how much comfort Buddy would provide. Just a few weeks later, our long-time cat, Snowflake, became very ill. Quickly, we took her to the vet, but she passed away, and we all missed her very much. But thank God for Buddy! He brought sunshine during those dark days.

"For the Lord God is a sun and shield: the Lord will give grace and glory: no good thing will he withhold from them that walk uprightly" (Psalm 84:11 KJV).

THE CAMERA CAT

When COVID-19 restrictions were in place for churches in West Virginia, my son revived the church with YouTube videos. The Big Four P.H. Church went on YouTube and continued this service. It benefits people who cannot attend church services, and those who live too far to come to the church.

I found out that I was not alone as I spoke on YouTube. Another cat saw the opportunity to pose for many people. Her name is Snickers. She jumps into a vacant seat beside me and looks straight into the camera.

Most of the time, she will sit still throughout the entire sermon, but sometimes, she smiles and purrs at the camera. Viewers comment that they enjoy seeing her. Like Snickers, people are encouraged to take time to listen to God's Word.

THE CAT WHO IS A FRIEND

"A man that has friends must show himself friendly: and there is a friend that sticks closer than a brother" (Proverbs 18:24 KJV).

Cole is a cat who is a friend to the other cats. He's well-mannered and patient and waits his turn to eat and play in the cat tunnel. Cole never steals the spotlight from the other cats.

Through Cole's behavior, we can learn about the fruit of the Spirit.

"But the fruit of the Spirit is love, joy, peace, longsuffering, gentleness, goodness, faith, meekness, temperance: against such there is no law" (Galatians 5:22 23 KJV).

PSALM 23

This psalm is a favorite of God's people. God's love for us is compared to the love a shepherd has for his sheep. The shepherd develops a close connection with the sheep.

"The Lord is my shepherd, I shall not want" (Psalm 23:1 KJV).

As mentioned earlier, I accompanied my grandfather as he

cared for the sheep. They belonged to a certain shepherd, and they knew his voice.

You may have heard of the stories of shepherds gathering their flocks, where all the sheep would be mixed together. But how would each shepherd identify his own sheep? As it was time to leave, each shepherd would venture off in a different direction and call out to his sheep. Amazingly, the sheep would recognize the voice of their own shepherd and follow them without fail.

Certainly, this is a lesson for us. Through times of prayer and waiting upon the Lord, we learn to follow His lead. And He promises that we shall not want.

The good shepherd leads his sheep into green pastures and beside still waters. We can trust God to take us to places of provision. All we have to do is ask.

PROTECTION

The good shepherd goes to great measures to protect his sheep. First of all, he counts them every day. I remember my grandfather counting the sheep in the mornings and evenings.

Jesus told a parable about the shepherd seeking the lost sheep.

"Suppose one of you has a hundred sheep and loses one of them. Doesn't he leave the ninety-nine in the open country and go after the lost sheep until he finds it?" (Luke 15:4 KJV).

THE SHEPHERD'S ROD

Shepherds use rods for several purposes. The rod can become a weapon to defend the sheep from predators. It can be used to warn the sheep to get back to the place of safety. Also, the shepherd may use his rod when counting the sheep.

A staff is similar to the rod, except it has a curved end. With the crook of the staff, the shepherd lifts a lamb that has wandered. He brings the lamb back to its mother. Also, he may use the crook of the rod to pull a sheep from a thorny bush.

"Yea, though I walk through the valley of the shadow of death, I will fear no evil; for thou art with me; thy rod and thy staff they comfort me" (Psalm 23:4 KJV).

ANOINTS WITH OIL

Shepherds pour special oil upon the heads of the sheep. This oil deters flies and parasites from irritating the sheep. Without the oil, the sheep are subject to inflammation and irritation from flies and parasites. Likewise, God, the Good Shepherd, anoints us, His sheep, to protect us from evil spirits.

"How God anointed Jesus of Nazareth with the Holy Ghost and with power: who went about doing good, and healing all that were oppressed of the devil; for God was with him" (Acts 10:38 KJV).

ONLY GOODNESS AND MERCY

The Good Shepherd takes such good care of His sheep that they can be assured of goodness and mercy following them.

Evil cannot follow them. These sheep trust the One who treats them well.

"Surely goodness and mercy shall follow me all the days of my life: and I will dwell in the house of the Lord forever" (Psalm 23:6 KJV).

CHAPTER 8

A SCENE FROM
THE COURTS IN HEAVEN

A couple of years before the COVID-19 pandemic, I saw a legal case being pleaded in the courts of heaven. It surprised me to see this. I had been praying about a career change, and I spent time in prayer and fasting about this issue. I was looking for answers, and this heavenly scene confirmed the direction I was to take.

I heard a voice saying, "Destruction!" The heavenly being said something like this: "But what about the destruction that is to come?"

The heavenly being was pleading a case for me and my family. I saw the heavenly being standing up and speaking for me. I was going to be given a choice. If I changed careers, my family would face destruction.

What did he mean by destruction? What about words such as "devastation" or "disaster"? These words were not used. Destruction awaited me if I made the wrong choice.

I did not realize the COVID-19 pandemic would be the destruction mentioned in the courts of heaven. Even though I did not understand, I was grateful for the chance. Scripture tells us to plead our cases before the Lord.

"Remind Me (of your merits with a thorough report), let us plead and argue our case together; State your position, that you may be proved right" (Isaiah 43:26 AMP).

That court scene I saw in heaven made me realize just how important it is to pray about our decisions!

TIMES TO HIDE

As I continued to study, I learned that there were times to hide.

Elijah the prophet, was a great example of hiding. During the famine, he hid by the brook called Cherith. He drank from the brook, and God sent ravens to bring him bread and flesh in the morning and evening (1 Kings 17:2-7).

Elijah stayed hidden until the brook dried up. At this point, God sent him to visit the widow of Zarephath (1 Kings 17:8-16).

HIDING FROM KING AHAB

For many days, Elijah hid from King Ahab. He stayed undercover until he received new instructions from the Lord.

"And it came to pass after many days, that the word of the Lord came to Elijah in the third year, saying, Go, show yourself unto Ahab; and I will send rain upon the earth" (1 Kings 18:1 KJV).

HIDE IN YOUR CHAMBER

A study of this scripture suggests that the Lord allowed judgment upon the land possibly because of violence and idolatry in Ahab's kingdom. The narrative continues to suggest that the Lord will punish Leviathan, the piercing servant.

"Come, my people, enter thou into thy chambers, and shut thy doors about thee: hide thyself as it were for a little moment, until the indignation be overpast" (Isaiah 26:20 KJV).

INFORMATION ABOUT THE REASONS FOR JUDGMENT

"For, behold, the Lord comes out of his place to punish the inhabitants of the earth for their iniquity: the earth also shall disclose her blood, and shall no more cover her slain" (Isaiah 26:21 KJV).

LEVIATHAN

The punishment of the Lord is also intended for Leviathan, a symbolic monster of the sea. Often, he is referred to as that crooked servant, dragon, or even Satan.

"In that day the Lord will punish Leviathan the fleeing serpent With His fierce and great and mighty sword (rescuing Israel from her enemy), Even Leviathan the twisted serpent; And He will kill the dragon who lives in the sea" (Isaiah 27:1 AMP).

Apparently, during this time of punishment for evil, God's people were to remain in their chambers. They were to shut their doors and hide. They were to stay hidden until the judgment was over. Scripture suggests that it would be "for a little moment" (Isaiah 26:20 KJV)

NOAH HIDES IN THE ARK

Noah and his family were in the ark for a little over a year. (Genesis 7:11-13, 8:14-20). Also, they had to wait for the waters to recede before it was safe to exit the ark.

Judgment came on the land in the form of water. Some of the

sins of mankind that brought God's anger were evil imaginations, violence, and wrong sexual relations (Genesis 6:1-8).

HIDE DURING EVIL RULERS

"When the wicked rise, men hide themselves: but when they perish, the righteous increase" (Proverbs 28:28 KJV).

The scriptures tell us that at times hiding is the wise thing to do.

ANOTHER CHANCE FOR KING HEZEKIAH

God is in the business of giving second chances. I was glad to receive a second chance to change my career choice. Otherwise, I would have plunged into a line of work that was high risk for COVID-19 exposure.

King Hezekiah became very ill. He was near the point of death. The Lord sent Isaiah the prophet to speak to the king. He was told to put his house in order because he would die. But King Hezekiah did not accept this verdict. He turned his face toward the wall and prayed. The king reminded God that he had a heart for Him, and he had helped steer the nation toward Him (Isaiah Chapter 38).

A NEW VERDICT FROM HEAVEN

Good news came from heaven. God told Isaiah to return to the king with a different message. The king's prayer saved his life.

"Go, and say to Hezekiah, 'Thus says the Lord, the God of David thy father, I have heard thy prayer, I have seen thy tears: behold, I will add unto thy days fifteen years" (Isaiah 38:5 KJV).

COMMIT YOUR WAY

"Commit your way unto the Lord; trust also in him; and he shall bring it to pass" (Psalm 37:5 KJV).

This scripture encourages us all to pray. Prayer can help us stay on the right path and steer clear of negative influences. By inviting God to intervene in our situations, we are closer to positive outcomes.

THE FUTURE

When we pray, we must remember that God knows what is going to occur in the future. We must trust Him in the present and future, even when we can't see the outcome.

HOW DO WE PRAY DURING COVID-19?

Often, during COVID-19, I felt lost as I prayed for our families, our region, and our nation. I clearly remember the Passover season in the year 2020. The report from the news was that over half a million people had died within three months.

Here was Passover season, and death was all around us!

I believed the United States and the entire world were experiencing a time of judgment. And I was eager to learn what the Scriptures taught about such times.

How did the people in the Bible pray during judgment?

How did the people respond to seasons of judgment?

What did the Bible say about plagues?

DIFFERENT VIEWS

As a thankful citizen of the United States, I respected the different viewpoints about COVID-19. Some churches did not seem to think it was a threat. Other churches took measures to protect their congregations. But the fact was that if you were in the wrong place at the wrong time, you could become a victim. Statistics proved this repeatedly. It was appalling that so much false information was spread.

I HAD TO LEARN TO PRAY ABOUT THIS ISSUE

I searched the Scriptures for new prayers and the Holy Spirit led me to key scriptures that I needed to pray daily.

ASK FOR WISDOM

As a pastor, COVID-19 presented great challenges. Our church is located in West Virginia, and the Governor of the state closed down all churches for a period of time. Therefore, we had to learn to reach people in new ways. Technology was the answer for us.

Our son worked long hours to get us on YouTube, and we posted sermons weekly. The church members were glad to hear a sermon from their church and participation on YouTube was very good. The members invited their families and friends and nearly every Sunday, about 25 to 40 people viewed the sermons. In addition, there was a "giving link" on the Big Four P. H. Church's YouTube channel.

I learned to pray for wisdom throughout all phases of the pandemic.

"If any of you lack wisdom, let him ask of God, that gives to all men liberally, and upbraids not; and it shall be given to him" (James 1:5 KJV).

A PRUDENT MAN

A thorough study of the Scriptures revealed much about COVID-19, and I truly wanted to know what the Word of God had to say about this issue. Such a study would help me pray more effectively.

"A prudent man foresees the evil, and hides himself: but the simple pass on, and are punished" (Proverbs 22:3 KJV).

This was a time in history when we should have strived to be on the side of the wise, not on the side of the simple. Being prudent meant not ignoring the danger but making proper preparations for any type of travel or interaction. Prudence also meant encouraging efforts to protect other people.

ESCAPES FROM DEATH

Another prayer that I learned to pray during the pandemic was for God to provide "escapes from death." I wanted God's protection for myself and my family, and I was humble enough to ask for it.

Surely there were scriptures available to confirm these prayers.

"God is to us a God of acts of salvation; And to God the Lord

133

belong escapes from death (setting us free). Surely God will shatter the head of His enemies" (Psalm 68:20, 21 AMP).

This was an important scripture for me because you never really knew where death might await during COVID-19.

Somebody needed to talk about the issue of death during this time. It was a common occurrence. All you had to do was turn on the television, and you would see cities, towns, and regions where deaths were numerous.

I am sure I was not the only one with the question:

WHY ARE SO MANY PEOPLE DYING?

Would the church address this issue? Would the church reach out with hope? This was a perfect chance for the church to step up.

Some ministers preached about these topics in a manner supported by scripture, and they gave me encouragement. However, this was also an ideal time for false prophets to emerge. I have never seen so many false prophets before! They prophesied events that never occurred and spoke on every available media platform. Along with death, there was an abundance of deception.

AFTER JUDGMENT

After judgment ends, there are certain actions that intercessors should take. A proper response can usher in a fresh wave of God's mercy and prevent further waves of judgment. Noah provides us with examples of how to respond after a judgment.

Finally, the time came for Noah and his family to depart from the ark. As previously mentioned, they had been on the ark for just over a year.

STEP ONE: THE RIGHT TIME

Noah waited on God's instructions and did not rush off the ark. I am sure they were "bursting with emotions" to get out.

"And God spoke to Noah, saying, 'Go out of the ark, you and your wife and your sons and their wives with you. Bring out with you every living thing from all flesh—birds and animals and every crawling thing that crawls on the earth---that they may breed abundantly on the earth, and be fruitful and multiply on the earth" (Genesis 8:15-17 AMP).

STEP TWO: THE RIGHT PLACE

God had provided a secure place for Noah and his family, where they could cultivate the land and prosper (Genesis 9:20).

In the present time, there is also a place for intercessors, called the secret place of the Most High, which is found in the shadow of the Almighty (Psalm 91:1). Intercessors must return to this place, put aside all distractions, repent of personal sins, and return to their calling. It is time to pray, pray, pray!

STEP THREE: THE RIGHT RESPONSE

One of the first things that Noah did was build an altar. What is an altar? It is a place to meet God. It is a place for the supernatural power of God to intervene in the earthly realm.

Noah was a man of prayer. He did not just pray every now and then. He was consistent in his prayer life. And God's presence showed up when Noah came to the altar!

"And Noah built an altar to the Lord, and took of every (ceremonially) clean animal and of every clean bird and offered burnt offerings on the altar" (Genesis 8:20 AMP).

Jesus was the ultimate sacrifice on the cross. Our sacrifices are no longer animals but repentance from a true heart.

"The sacrifices of God are a broken spirit: a broken and a contrite heart, O God, thou wilt not despise" (Psalm 51:17 KJV).

King David is the person in this scripture who offers repentance. He models the condition of a real heart of repentance!

GOD RESPONDS

Our prayers should receive a positive response from heaven. Often, I ask for confirmation that my prayers were heard!

"The Lord smelled the pleasing aroma (a soothing, satisfying scent) and the Lord said to Himself, I will never again curse the ground because of man, for the intent (strong inclination, desire) of man's heart is wicked from his youth, and I will never again destroy every living thing, as I have done" (Genesis 8:21 AMP).

Where are the altars to God in the post-pandemic world? Is the sweet aroma of prayer ascending to the heavens?

A PRAYER FOR LIGHT

Your lovingkindness and graciousness, O Lord, extend to the skies, Your faithfulness (reaches) to the clouds. Your righteousness is like the mountains of God, Your judgments are like the great deep. O LORD, You preserve man and beast. How precious is Your lovingkindness, O God! The children of men take refuge in the shadow of Your wings. They drink their fill of the abundance of Your house; And You allow them to drink from the river of Your delights. For with You is the fountain of life (the fountain of life-giving water); in your light we see light. (Psalm 36:5–9 AMP)

IN YOUR LIGHT WE SEE LIGHT!

ABOUT THE AUTHOR

Mary Donna Hankla appreciates her husband and son. Both provide vital support for the ministry. Donna has been licensed and ordained as a minister with the International Pentecostal Holiness Church (IPHC) for 22 years. She serves in the Appalachian Conference as a pastor and the director of World-Wide Intercessory Network known as WIN.

Donna has been a participant in several key prayer movements. These include a 24-hour prayer event hosted by Capitol Hill Prayer Partners. She led a team during prayer watches over various days and nights for this prayer initiative.

Night watch prayer yearly is also hosted by Capitol Hill Prayer Partners. Each year, Donna recruited intercessors to cover night prayer for a period of three weeks. She also participated in all-night prayer meetings.

For 15 years, Donna led a team from the Appalachian Conference to Washington, D.C. for the National Day of Prayer. The prayer team joined other prayer groups from the nation. Prayers were offered for the nation and Israel.

With the shofar, and shouts of victory, Donna has led several prayer walks to key places such as Mount Mitchell. Prayers were made to protect the United States.

Since the year 2007, Donna has been pastoring at the Big Four P.H. Church in Kimball, WV.

Currently, Donna works with a community action group to assist pregnant mothers, and children to the age of three.

Mary Donna Hankla can be followed on her Author Central webpage at:
https://www.amazon.com/author/marydonnahankla

141

www.ingramcontent.com/pod-product-compliance
Lightning Source LLC
Chambersburg PA
CBHW060538130626
46553CB00002B/803

9 798988 039402